The S Gobbler and other stories

Contents

The Sock Gobbler

by Barbara Berge
illustrated by Emma Priest

Brent's neighbour, Mr Forbes, was watching Brent on his skateboard. "That's an interesting pair of socks you're wearing," he said. Brent was wearing one red sock with blue stripes and one green sock with yellow stripes. "Have you got another pair like that at home?"

"No," said Brent. "I've got a lot of socks, but none of them are the same."

"Why not?" asked Mr Forbes.

"The sock gobbler eats them," said Brent.

Mr Forbes looked surprised. "Where does this sock gobbler live?"

"In our washing machine."

"Why do you think it only eats one sock out of each pair?" asked Mr Forbes.

"I don't know," Brent shrugged. "I suppose it gets bored after the first one. I'm going to set a trap for it tonight. Then maybe Mum'll believe me."

That night, Brent stayed awake. When at last everyone had gone to bed, he tiptoed out of his bedroom and went downstairs. With his heart beating wildly, he crept up to the washing machine. He lifted the lid and quickly dropped in a pair of his sister's socks. They were her best pink ones, with red strawberries around the top. He waited quietly to see what happened.

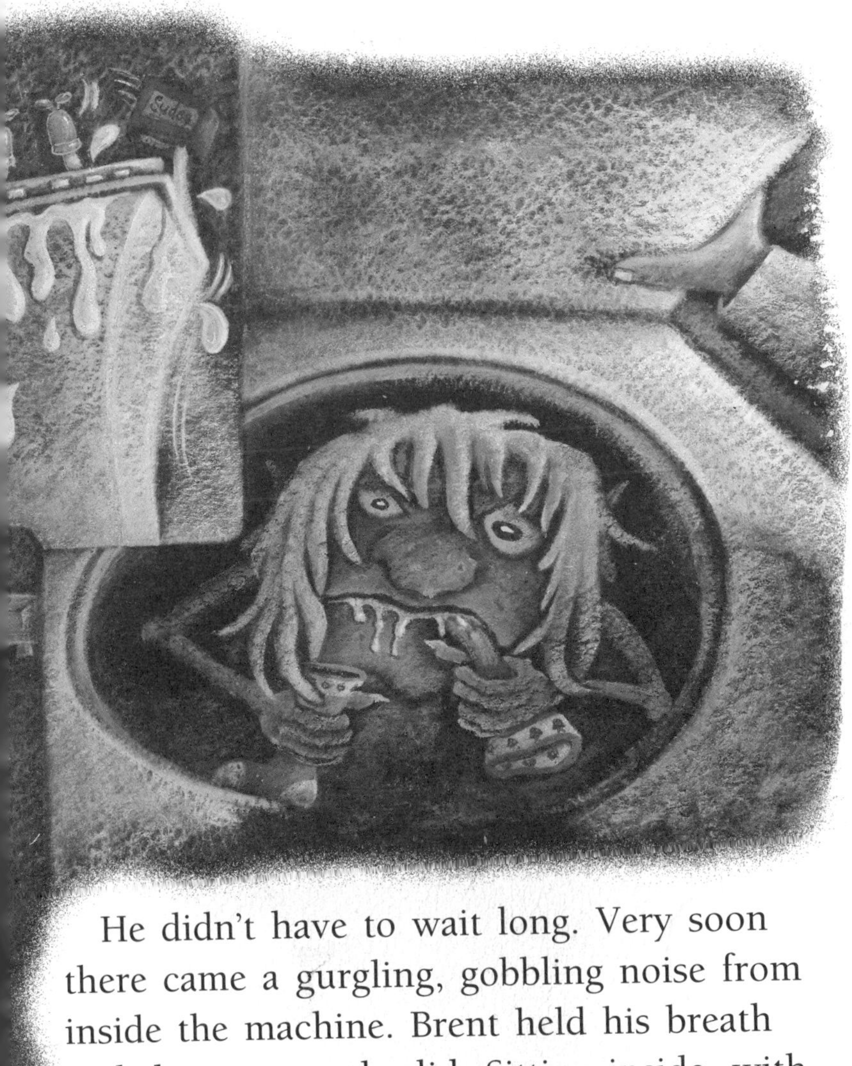

He didn't have to wait long. Very soon there came a gurgling, gobbling noise from inside the machine. Brent held his breath and threw open the lid. Sitting inside, with one of the pink socks in its enormous mouth, was … the sock gobbler!

Brent and the sock gobbler stared at each other. The sock gobbler was a browny-greeny colour with long, skinny arms and legs. A woolly mane draggled over its grimy face, and it smelled like sweaty feet. Its strange, yellow eyes glared up out of the washing machine.

Suddenly it burped and dived back down. But it had eaten too much. It was stuck, and its legs were waving around in the air.

Brent grabbed hold of one skinny leg. But the sock gobbler was slimy, and Brent had to fight hard to hold on. He pulled and pulled while a slobbering, gobbling noise came from inside the washing machine.

All at once there was an enormous SCHLOP as the sock gobbler flew out of the machine and landed in a heap on top of Brent.

"Ouch!" cried Brent. "That hurt!"

The sock gobbler was already running off up the hall. Brent was just in time to see it disappear under his bed. It hid there, giggling to itself.

"You can stay there, then," Brent told it. "Just wait till my mum sees you in the morning!"

"Wake up, sleepyhead," said Brent's mother, shaking him gently. "You'll be late for school."

Brent's head felt a bit fuzzy. Suddenly he remembered what was under his bed. "Mum, guess what?" he cried. "I caught the sock gobbler. It's under my bed!"

"Come on, Brent," said his mother. "You've had another bad dream."

"No, Mum, it's true!" Brent leaped out of bed. "Look," he said.

They both peered under the bed.

"Oh, Brent," sighed his mother. Shaking her head, she returned to the kitchen.

The sock gobbler had gone. Under Brent's bed was a small piece of pink material and the smell of dirty socks.

Later, when Brent passed the washing machine, he heard a chuckle and a burp.

"I'll get you," he whispered.

"What did you say?" asked his mother.

"Nothing," said Brent.

SOCKS

Red socks and yellow socks,
purple socks and pink.
Clean socks and not-so-clean
and socks that really stink.

Striped socks and spotted socks
and socks with lace and bows.
Long socks and short socks
and socks with holey toes.

Socks! Socks! So many socks!
I've got socks to spare.
But, however hard I look,
I can never find a pair!

by Jane Buxton
illustrated by Fifi Colston

The Real World

by Alan Bagnall
illustrated by Philip Webb

When we came home from school, Mum was dreaming in the garden. So we ran into the kitchen and dumped our backpacks.

At that *very* moment, a giant stomped in behind us – a huge, hairy giant from the hills.

"I'm hungry," growled the giant. "In fact, I'm starving!"

"Hold on, Giant – wipe your feet!" I scolded. "You've left mud all over the floor!"

"I'm ravenous!" boomed the giant. "I could eat everything in this house!"

"There are no biscuits left," Kelly said, showing the giant an empty tin. "You'll have to cook something."

"I can't," moaned the giant. "I don't know how to cook."

Kelly shrugged.

"You!" He pointed to Kelly. "You cook for me!"

"OK, then, Giant. What would you like?"

"Pancakes!"

We all rushed to help. We made a pancake as big as the pan.

The giant ate it in three bites.

"More!" he cried, grabbing the bag of flour. "More pancakes!"

He spilled flour everywhere. It all got trampled into the mud on the floor.

At last, after six pancakes, the giant was satisfied.

"Thanks a million, kids. Great pancakes! I'll come again!" And the giant stomped out and away, back to the hills, with bits of pancake stuck in his whiskers.

Then Mum came in from dreaming in the garden. She got wild when she saw the kitchen. She wouldn't believe us about the giant, and she made us clean up all the mess he'd made.

That's the whole trouble with mothers. They just don't live in **the real world.**

What I Did in the Holidays

by Marion Rego
illustrated by Sarah Farman

Mr Wilson thinks I'm writing a story. I've got my book in front of me and my pencil in my hand. Everyone else is writing away, and I'm trying to look as if I'm busy too.

But I don't like writing stories. I can never think of anything interesting.

Mr Wilson said to write about what we did in the holidays. But I didn't do anything in the holidays. It was boring. So I don't know what to write. Maybe I'll just make something up.

I could say **I went to South America and sailed down the Amazon on a riverboat**. The jungle came right down to the edge of the water, and I could see monkeys swinging around in the trees. I didn't go ashore because I might have been grabbed by a python and swallowed whole. And I had to be careful not to fall in the river – the piranhas would have gobbled me up till there was nothing left but a skeleton.

gobble
gobble

Or maybe **I went to the Antarctic and made my way by dog sled to the south pole**, day after day over the ice and snow. Halfway back, we were caught in a blizzard and had to shelter in our tiny tent. We were nearly out of food and were just about down to our last biscuit when the blizzard stopped.

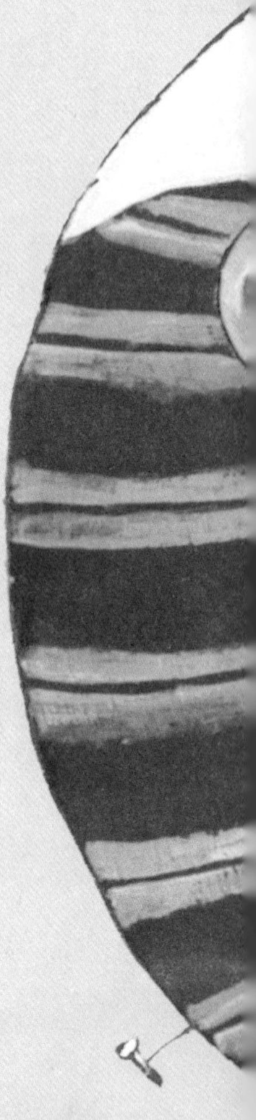

I'd better write something. What about being **the first person to land on Mars**? That would really be something. Maybe there were other people living there already. And they grabbed hold of me, and I said, "Take me to your leader."

So they did, and he had eyes on stalks on the top of his head, and an X-ray eye in the middle of his forehead, and he said, "You're just the person I've been waiting to see. I've got a job that only an earth person can do." **Only how did he learn to speak English if I was the first earth person to go there?**

Back to earth. Here comes Mr Wilson. He thinks I'm working. **Maybe I'd better start.**

Just One Thing

by K.E. Anderson
illustrated by Donna Cross

Mrs Funnell is famous for telling stories. She's the best storyteller in the whole school.

On Monday, Mrs Funnell was telling a story about how she used to be a pirate captain before she was a schoolteacher.

She had her old pirate scarf on and her pirate eyepatch, and she held a treasure map in her hand. Out of her pocket poked the handle of a pirate pistol. It was made from gold and silver and was covered with red and green and blue jewels.

"Just then," said Mrs Funnell, "a cannon ball crashed right through the bow of my ship, and we started to sink. My crew were so terrified that they all jumped overboard into shark-infested water."

"It was a terrible sight. I grabbed my spyglass and peered out over the ocean. Not too far away I saw a tiny island, so I rushed to my cabin. The boat was sinking fast, so I only had time to put one thing in my pocket before I jumped into the longboat and rowed to the island. With this one thing I knew I would be rescued."

"What was it?" asked Blair.

"Would anyone like to guess?" asked Mrs Funnell. "Ellen?"

"Some matches so you could start a fire to attract attention?"

"Good guess," said Mrs Funnell. "But no, I didn't take any matches with me."

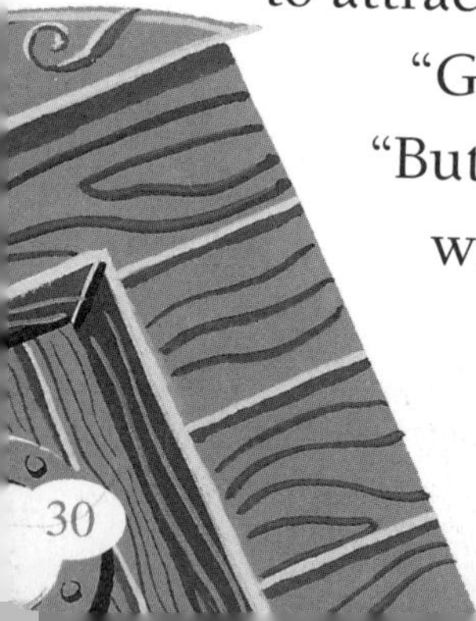

"A mirror so you could reflect the sun off it and get the attention of passing ships?" suggested Blair.

Mrs Funnell smiled. "Good thinking, but no, I didn't take a mirror with me."

"Did you take your spyglass and use the glass to make a fire to signal with?" asked Tracey.

"Hey," said Mrs Funnell, "you would all make amazing pirates. But no, I lost my spyglass overboard as I jumped into the longboat."

Suddenly Colin had an idea. "Did you quickly write a message while you were in your cabin, put it in a bottle, and throw it into the sea?"

"Great idea, Colin, but no, I didn't put a message in a bottle."

The class had run out of ideas.

"Would you like me to tell you what I took with me?" asked Mrs Funnell.

The whole class nodded.

"My mobile phone," said Mrs Funnell, taking it out of her pocket. "All I had to do was ring the emergency services, and I was rescued at once by the coastguard."

On Tuesday, when the children arrived at school, Mrs Funnell was wearing her astronaut suit ...